THE PORTAGE POETRY SERIES

Series Titles

Sadness of the Apex Predator
Dion O'Reilly

The Trouble with Being a Childless Only Child
Michelle Meyer

Happy Everything
Caitlin Cowan

Dear Lo
Brady Bove

Don't Feed the Animal
Hikari Miya

Glitter City
Bonnie Jill Emanuel

Listening to Mars
Sally Ashton

The Watching Sky
Judy Brackett Crowe

Let It Be Told in a Single Breath
Russell Thorburn

The Blue Divide
Linda Nemec Foster

Lake, River, Mountain
Mark B. Hamilton

Talking Diamonds
Linda Nemec Foster

Poetic People Power
Tara Bracco (ed.)

The Found Object Imagines a Life: New and Selected Poems
Mary Catherine Harper

Naming the Ghost
Emily Hockaday

Mourning
Dokubo Melford Goodhead

Messengers of the Gods: New and Selected Poems
Kathryn Gahl

After the 8-Ball
Colleen Alles

Careful Cartography
Devon Bohm

Broken On the Wheel
Barbara Costas-Biggs

Sparks and Disperses
Cathleen Cohen

Holding My Selves Together: New and Selected Poems
Margaret Rozga

Lost and Found Departments
Heather Dubrow

Marginal Notes
Alfonso Brezmes

The Almost-Children
Cassondra Windwalker

Meditations of a Beast
Kristine Ong Muslim

Praise for

Sadness of the Apex Predator

"Dion O'Reilly's *Sadness of the Apex Predator* is a tour de force with urgent poems that address the perilous present and the past that's gotten us here. She writes astonishing poems of her personal history of severe abuse and world history of severe abuse. She even contemplates poets taking 'a break/from our ruined selves/in favor of our ruined country.' A burn survivor, O'Reilly writes visceral poems addressing not only the pain but also vulnerability—'I had no skin./I'm sorry. I had no skin.' In later poems she returns to the body—its pleasure and difficulties. These are wonderful and necessary poems."

—Denise Duhamel
author of *Second Story*

"Dion O'Reilly's brilliant book *Sadness of the Apex Predator* simply can't be contained in a short comment. There's an entire world here, as well as the history of beauty and unspeakable brutality of which the human animal is equally capable. The poems are searingly vivid, public, political, but also intensely and painfully intimate. O'Reilly moves effortlessly between the lyric and demotic, a whisper building to a scream and back again. And always the wondrous, leaping nerve of O'Reilly's language here. Image after image completely floored me. This is one of my favorite books in recent memory. What a voice."

—Erin Bilieu
author of *Come-Hither Honeycomb*

"In *Sadness of the Apex Predator*, a girl-child withdraws into a scar-riddled body, a space safe from a mother's whip, where she takes refuge in the 'proper hush and flow machine' of her own body until she is ready to face a world that preys on her. With language both muscular and merciless, O'Reilly debrides aggression from the newfound body of her speaker. She lays bare some very hard truths, yet these are poems that teach foremost of decency, cautioning us to wean ourselves of the hindbrain's instinct to inflict harm, of the impulse to place ourselves first."

—Rooja Mohassessy
author of *When Your Sky Runs Into Mine*

"The poems in Dion O'Reilly's *Sadness of the Apex Predator* leap off the page with ruthless, unsparing language. In brilliantly sharp sestinas, pantoums, and stanzaic forms, Dion O'Reilly lays bare the pathetic nature of cruelty and how enormous an abusive mother is to a child: 'When my mother threw encyclopedias at us / she threw the world.' The poems root into questions about love, girlhood, and sexuality with startling honesty and show that child abuse persists long after childhood ends 'How many times have I returned / to a mother who savaged me? / Searched for her again and again // in the bodies of men.' Too often we turn away from the brutality of the domestic realm, yet these poems put it starkly front and center. I was entirely absorbed by their visceral beauty. I think O'Reilly is writing some of the most compelling poems out there."

—Jessica Cuello
editor of *Tahoma Review*
author of *Dear Creature*

SADNESS OF THE APEX PREDATOR

poems   DION O'REILLY

CORNERSTONE PRESS
UNIVERSITY OF WISCONSIN-STEVENS POINT

ererer Harererararar

Cornerstone Press, Stevens Point, Wisconsin 54481
Copyright © 2024 Dion O'Reilly
www.uwsp.edu/cornerstone

Printed in the United States of America by
Point Print and Design Studio, Stevens Point, Wisconsin

Library of Congress Control Number: 2023950494
ISBN: 978-1-960329-27-1

Cover art: "Big Fish Eat Little Fish," a 1557 engraving by Pieter van der Heyden
from Pieter Bruegel's 1556 drawing | Harris Brisbane Dick Fund, 1917

Cornerstone Press titles are produced in courses and internships offered by the
Department of English at the University of Wisconsin–Stevens Point.

DIRECTOR & PUBLISHER
Dr. Ross K. Tangedal

EXECUTIVE EDITORS
Jeff Snowbarger, Freesia McKee

EDITORIAL DIRECTOR
Ellie Atkinson

SENIOR EDITORS
Brett Hill, Grace Dahl

PRESS STAFF
Carolyn Czerwinski, Chloe Cieszynski, Sophie McPherson, Natalie Reiter, Ava Willett

To Arthur, Darrian, Logan, and Owen

CONTENTS

1.

2.

3.

4.

1.

There Was Smoke in the Sunrise

It glitzed the vinyl floor
an oxblood hue. Outside a clatter
in the naked snag, crow calls
like stilettos on blacktop. For years
they've been warning us—
black Cassandras of the powerlines.

It's sad, really, how pain teaches
truth, as if it knows something
we need to learn.
The ending should be simple—
the fox choked on chicken feathers,
the wolf slit open, the eaten freed.

How I love a campfire story—
my face hot from the blaze,
my back blained with cold—
behind me, the tangled trees,
the endless dark, so many ravenous
creatures I can't see.

World Books

When my mother threw encyclopedias at us,
she threw the world: mammals of North America,
Doric columns and eggplants, giraffe necks,
bustles, empire dresses; pale, pushed-up breasts.
She threw colorplates of striped beetles. She threw The Beatles,
hot air balloons, the race to the moon, Jackie's pill hat,
the putative curse of communism. She threw staked
witches of the Inquisition, gray-toned photos
of bristlecone pines like Old Testament prophets pointing to the sky.
The books winged like startled doves, fluttered scattershot
into my father's face, the back of my head, my sister's lumbar.
Oh, *World Books*, implements of a mother's fits, her unread
history, uncracked cipher, unseen Rosetta. Her Gnostic Gospel
rotting in a Coptic jar.

Tools

My grandfather loved Victor traps.
My grandmother—a sow-bug vacuum cleaner,
zoetropes, a set of wooden spoons.

My father loved his roll-top desk,
crank adding machine, books
by Sinclair Lewis and Lewis Browne.

For Mr. Davenport—the man who sheared the sheep—
hemp ropes to hog-tie, a razor to shave them,
slash their pink skin on purpose,
while he raved that Jews controlled the banks.

Stay in the house, Mother told my Jewish father
when she saw Davenport's truck
barrel down the driveway
like a loose bull.

Back then, I thought all tools were human—
the mind picked the tool
to fit the mind.
The tool shaped the mind.

But sorrow, sorrow was animal.

The soft, frantic lambs with thick, shitty coats,
fragrant of grass and body heat,
baaed like babies beneath the blade.

Job done, they struggled to their feet,
shivered, their bodies covered
in ruby slits like little mouths.

Davenport sheathed his hand shear
in its ringed belt. It sounded
like ice on ice.

Roots

...i mean any word
traced to its origin is a small child begging for water.
—sam sax

The few things that killed us
when we lived in trees—
snakes coiled in branches,
falling, others of our kind,

whatever we find out about ourselves
under mounds in the jungle—
stone beds of the dead, grooved
with runnels to carry blood,
obsidian knives to slice
through breastbones, lift
our slippery hearts to the sun,

certain smells like petrol and bitumen,
toxic and appealing,
the sadness of orphaned prairies—
switchgrass and sideoats
still alive under fences,
seed heads in front of a plow
like gloved hands waving *Goodbye. Goodbye.*

* * *

Constantine changing his mind,
the angel Jibrīl
lighting up a cave,

a herd miles wide,
piled into bones,
a blanket of fat pigeons
in the sky
we wanted to prick with light,

an archduke and duchess, shot,
mushroom clouds
lifting their gorgeous heads,

layered gelatin sparkling
in compote glass
that made a Boer decide
on Apartheid.

* * *

Memories of my mother's rough palms
that she spat on
to clean my face, the smell
of her spit,

the thousand ways I was taught
to smile and shake hands, words falling
like family china from my fingers,
the yellowy photos of broken men
I loved, knowing they ruined my children,
my children's pain displacing my own:

the biggest lie about the past
is that it's past—
the present, a wall
to keep history from swarming
the future.

Watch, as you lean against the redwood,
the starling-flits, their flying matched
to any music you can think of,

a million roots below you
sending out fingers
to touch other trees.

Presidential Campaign 2020

When I think of a mongrel dog
like Laika, sent up with Sputnik,
it's difficult for me to believe
there's any goodness
worth voting for. Not even Biden
who Old-Guards swear "will restore
decency to America," and whom
of course I will
vote for in an act of duty and desperation.

When I think of the hands, strapping that dog
into his small capsule, with a crap bag
and enough gel dog food to last a few days,
snapping the chains that let Laika stand
or sit or lie down, when I imagine
the dexterity of the human fingers
and the intelligence and cruelty,
I can hardly stand to look at Biden
who was only a football-playing high schooler
in 1957 and had nothing to do with Laika.

But before Laika was shot toward the sun,
a scientist brought him home
to play with his children,
and I think of any happy time before death
or during great torment as a gift
we can give to each other, to anyone,
just to do it, for no other reason
than the good need to give
because we realize we should

share whatever sanity or means we have
if we're decent human beings—
like that scientist, who may have calmed
the lifted hairs on the dog's back
as he lay in the tight chamber, smelling
that weird smell they say rockets have of
gunpowder, rum, and seared steak.

When I think of the countdown and the racket,
how that dog must have pushed against the chains and whined,
I feel a bit strapped-in myself, a bit like I'm hurtling
into something so much bigger, so much outside of the thin
circling rim of atmosphere, thin like my own thin skin
that could so easily be burned away,

and I can't help noticing Biden has strong hands
because he was a football player,
so he probably has those kind of fingers
that could pull in a pigskin
and run like hell and win.
I think he might caress and sniff
my hair and brilliant the world with his teeth
and I might lick his hand
if he were the one to care for me
on my last day
or in the midst of my chaining.
Yes, I might lick his hand
because I can smell his decency,
and I hope we can change our lives.

Okanogan 1980

Half the time, I was high on something
picked out of cowshit in the Skagit
or bought for fifteen bucks from a dodgy stranger.
But that day, nothing but a stack of pancakes,
bleeding blue from blackberries,
bought at a coffee shop in Marblemount.

In a field outside Tonasket, I saw
a drum, big as a trampoline—twelve Native men
stood round it. The one named Red swelled,
merged with the Cascades to the west.

He said he'd spied an egg in a ground nest,
its cracks caked with serum,
a yellow-bellied snake coiled round it—
half dead, flaking its skin.
The sound of pipping within
told him Mount St. Helens was about to blow.

The next Sunday, she did, as I drove
home through scrubby flatlands
scraped by glaciers, cataclysms,
rent valves of the earth—
all those traces of torments
I was too young to see.

That evening, I fell asleep in a field
I thought was empty, woke at midnight,
a train's roar gaining on me, thundering
through dirt to my body—six feet
from steel rails, invisible in the black,
the darkness lit by a single eye.

Confessional poetry is dead

is what I'm hearing everywhere—
the famous poet behind me
at the wine bar, for example,
says she no longer writes
about working as a janitor
in Saskatchewan, or leaving
her crying daughter on a swing set.
Maybe she's right.
Maybe we need a break
from our ruined selves
in favor of our ruined country.
All that toddler questioning—
Me. Me. Why? Why? That's over,
we're teenagers now—
our famous, invulnerable,
fifteen-year-old American self,
finally crushed in a dumb accident—
liberty, freedom, and you-can-be-
whoever-you-want-to-be—
a film negative of the truth,
Bizarro World, compensation
for a rigged system.
I'm sorry. I must confess again.
It's like a tic. I can't help myself.
I'm hurting because my mother
was a sadistic lunatic because her mother
was a passive aggressive lunatic,
because her mother had twelve dead babies
before her liver wasted away—
all of it, a huge secret

in our Perfect Rich White Nuclear family.
Perfect. Rich. White. Nuclear.
Are those words enough
for you to like me?
To hate me? For you to see
this pain I need to confess
is a small part
of something terribly broken.

Preference

My mother wanted me to find a man
with eyes like mine
to father my children,

perhaps because she prized her own
sapphire eyes, passed down to her
by a father who could break

an acre of wheat,
then lean on his spade
like a lord.

He had ocean eyes, fought Nazis in France,
kept a forty-five on his car seat,
taught me to oil a gun.

Maybe he thought my mother needed governance.
Maybe he beat her
before she learned to speak.

All I know is—
she was hell-bent
on his love.

Please don't misunderstand me—
I believed her, feared
the beauty of black-eyed men,

saw no danger in her desires,
never wondered where
the blue-eyed glamor began—

the centuries,
carried across oceans
in the bellies of tortured ships,

in fields of cotton and cane,
in mothers' hearts.

Plenty

August, the last of the apricots
haunts the trees. Their furred skins, split,
rotten and dangerous, crawling
with stingers on the unseen
side of the globes.
    Above me, buzzards tilt in the heat.
Do they miss the condors?
The stiff keratin of the bigger beak
to splay a corpse's flanks, break it
for a weaker brother.
    I heard we once crept
behind hyenas, cracked
the bones of their leavings,
squatted and sucked the soft insides.
    So many ghosts shimmer
the sky, shiver the leaves—
the ten thousand helpmates,
swarms of the world, whispering,
Let me feed my hunger first—
then you.

Big Fish Eat Little Fish

after a drawing by Pieter Bruegel the Elder, 1556

Flying fish pause mid-flight, watch the butchers
carve the whale-gut, disgorge her digestion—
smaller bodies, same as hers, swallowed whole.
They, in turn, puke minnows & krill, tinier still.

All feeding, all food, mindless, unmaliced, nothing else,
in tidal whispers, moon shifts, & blackness, but to open
her great unseen mouth, suck down what drifted in,
thick & slippery in schools.

The men bring hooks, tritons, ladders, boats, saws,
cities & cranes, wild instruments of dissection,
to slice up a deep-water creature, find the endless hunger there.

Maybe they recall—in their blood-warm bodies—
when sweet eaters of salmon sprouted feet from fins,
covered the earth, learned to be human.

2.

Helpless

Silence of a dog whistle.
Sky with a hole in it

a child fell through.

Don't you think it's useless
to save anyone? The little girl.

Is it a little girl?
Lying there like a dull knife,

like a spilled gallon of milk,
like a little girl

with a spray of freckles
across her cheekbones.

I place my palms on the wet
asphalt around her hair,

try to remember the ABCs
of keeping someone alive—

compression to the heart,
breath. The ground seems to throb.

I can barely see in this rain.

The man who bathed me in the burn ward

was middle-aged and patient
as a vulture.

And I? What was I?—a teenager
becoming something else, remnant
of a burnt-out house, uncured meat,
blood-fragment of a butchered bird.

He pulled me from my sticky bed each day—
no—twice a day. He was my morning
and night man,

lumbering lumberjack of a man, moon-faced
man with an unshaved neck,
wide-girthed man with careful hands.

He made me grateful for him—
tested the water, tepid to the wrist,
shorted the chlorine for me—
that alkaline wire in the water,
piranhas on the back skin,
razors peeling it.

He mixed it first, so it didn't whip
when it hit, lowered me gentle
into a robe of pain, plush pain, warm
reminder of that other
burning pain.

He cleaned me slow—
didn't seem to mind

my screams as he debrided
the collops and green clots.
His nemesis was the hungry sepsis
that ate me.

Why did it feel like love?
I was the buoyant creature
of his hand, strapping ranch-girl
who wasted and healed,
whose skin sucked life
from bones and fat
to lace the corset of flesh.

The grafts took, skin,
fragile as a winged thing curtained
down my back. And when I lay
naked in the final water,
he looked at me
like I was a tidbit,

told me he'd fixed me up
like a fat farm,
asked me to the movies.

What was he thinking?
Did he think I'd want him
now that I was whole?

Big Sister

Let's say she kept her promise, lifted me
from the tub.

Let's say she watched *Bonanza* and waited
as I scrubbed my sores, ran a flannel
over my wasted thighs—
the warts and moles, blemishes and fat
flamed away by fire.

Let's pretend she said, *I'm sorry*
when she dropped me, slammed my head
on the porcelain ridge—a deep ring
beginning in my ears.

I would have understood: it's difficult—
even for a grown woman—
to carry a wet, burned girl.

Let's say she tried again, and this time,
managed my slippery body,
toweled my florid scars, rib-ridges,
and vertebrae, threaded my arms
through the sleeves of a robe,

helped me to the couch, talked to me,
said she'd visit tomorrow
because my friends didn't know
what to do with me—
I couldn't take my skin to the beach,
couldn't feel my life beginning.

Let's say as I lay in the tub, dazed,
she didn't scream, *Look at you. I can't take it,*
didn't slam the door, leave me alone,
floor it up the driveway
in her beat up Rambler.

Let's say she wanted to lift me up,
but no one taught her how.

Let's say that.

Small Murders

I cut the mango my mother saved for me—
its leathery skin, wrinkled and freckled brown.
I offer her a slice, glistening
on the edge of the blade.

She says, *I just killed a rat
with that knife.*

She likes to share with me
her love of small murders. Carefully,
she taught me to clout rabbits' heads
with an iron pipe, slit their necks.

Then she left me to the work
of filling my lonely afternoons
with killing the litters,
smell of entrails and comfort
of making puppets, fitting my fingers
into the soft, inside-out pelts.

The dogs, finally, would amble
away to rest beneath the shrubs,
half-sick from crunching heads
thrown into their mouths.

Why does she find it pleasing
to see life flee a body?
The blind parakeet
whose throat she razored,
my elegant Great Dane,

his legs buckling
while she slapped his face.

She must like the clean
empty absence she makes
when she sends a soul away.

She sucks the flesh as I clean the knife.
The rat struggled, she says,
but I kept at it.

When I think of my sister's happiness

as she watched our mother strip me,
begged our father to beat me,
how she left me once, concussed,
in a tub, I want to feed her a scrap
of my own meat. She seemed so hungry,
so lit by the love of my blood.
Well, we were both hungry, though
we ate and ate. There was so much food. We were rich!
We stuffed clothes in our closets. Drove around
in a Lincoln. We had everything.
And then she grew breasts!
And Mummy loved her breasts!
They hunted boys with those breasts. Boys
in my sister's bed, boys on the blue leather
of the backseat. Boys with Mummy
eating jammy cookies at the table.
But I think my sister was still hungry
for me. Well, I was hungry for her. Hungry
for safety in a sister's arms,
someone to kiss me after a whipping.
There was a time she'd hold me like that.
She'd say, *Don't cry*, and untangle my hair.
She stopped the day our mother
pulled us apart, said, *Don't you dare*.
My sister was beautiful
under that bright kitchen light
as she turned away.
She seemed sad, but powerful.

Red Truck

I didn't want him—
surprise little brother
in the front seat
when I walked out of high school
on a hot day,

his tiny hand
smearing marks on the fancy
wood of the Mercedes dash,
the other pressed in the gold
cowhide of the front seat.

So small for four years old,
bitten up from the orphanage,
scratches on his face,
he leaned toward me,
said, *Hello Dion*—

He'd practiced all the way
from San Francisco,
where he was bought
from some downtown lawyer
for the price of a new Toyota
after the state agency refused.

My father sat in back, shoes off,
peeling dead skin off his feet,
mumbling a worn-out argument.
My mother—with parlor hair,
aquamarine eyes, smell of

Yardley Violets and antiperspirant—
smiled at the steering wheel.

What could I say? He was there
to save them. He clutched
a small red truck.
He knew my name.

Sister Sestina

Hard to believe,
once, all I wanted
was to be pretty,
to be loved.
My older sister's body
was made of men,

desire-drunk men
gilded with belief
in the pull-tide of her body.
I saw it so often, I wanted
it too. I was not loved,
only beaten, but I wanted to be pretty.

I knew I'd never be pretty,
never unravel men,
pull their love
from their throats, make them believe
what they wanted
was the ruby-heat of my body.

I was told a woman's body
was a sting, to be pretty,
a scorpion, to be wanted
by the ember-eyes of men—
a witch-made safety. I believed
what I was told about love,

but it bought me no love,
no light in the hollows of my body.

Back then, my sister believed
our mother's incantations—be pretty,
let your scent ensorcell men.
To be wanted

was all she wanted
Maybe because we were beaten, love
became the breath of men.
When our beaten bodies
lit them with panic, we felt pretty,
believed.

We didn't want to be sisters, only bodies,
safe from the whip, loved, pretty.
Men would split us like fruit. Believe us.

Closet

She wanted her father to stop her mother,
but he couldn't.

I suck my thumb and mess my pants,
she pleaded as he took her to private school
on his way to work—no breakfast,
her insides screaming, dressed
in the dirty shirt she slept in.

Still dark, the janitor let her in.
She'd wait in front of a burping heater,
nursing her thumb
till the rest arrived in a raucous wave.

*   *   *

On the ranch, she looked at the sun,
wondered if another world
spun on its far side.

She learned the language of crows
as they screamed in ravines,
heard teeth ticking the lawn
as Father mowed, mumbled,
softly cried.

*   *   *

Crouched in her closet, she studied
the vaulted architecture of her mind,

saw whole lives there, drew them by feel
on walls behind the clothes, pushed
her pencil into the wood, felt a shivering
contentment as she drew fairy tales, slowly
soiled herself, filled the air with stench.

*   *   *

No prince lived in her closet. Just me,
she whispered, and squeezed
her anal sphincter with the closest
she could get to pleasure—
holding back. Letting go.

What It Took

After I burned, my mother's life became nothing
but watching the blue of my eyes roll into darkness,

nothing but listening to the shudder of teeth
as they bloodied my tongue.

I became her baby again, gauze wrapped, just my face visible,
neck vein tapped for morphine like an umbilical.

Each day, when she walked through the burn room doors,
did she remember the night I emerged from her wet darkness,

before she ever lifted my skin with a lunge whip?

She watched, hands folded, as my salts leaked
from my unskinned back and legs, watched

as the white-gowned nurses rushed to fill me
with whatever liquid mineral my heart needed.

She watched the way mothers watch their babies—
        till their eyes burn.

Time in the Burn Ward

Maybe I split in two, witnessed my mind
like a fly on a broken clock.

Maybe the window, high up, let me watch the dusk
entered by night, buzzards

etching thin lines in the clouds, the flags
below me, cleaning their bucking sides in the wind.

Maybe my life was never mine. I only passed through it,
smudged by whatever I looked at or remembered—

daffodils, stained-glass wings of migrating monarchs,
my brother's eyes when he caught a spiral.

Maybe what snapped in me
was my hardness. I lengthened inside the pills,

learned the shiver-love of being threaded by IVs,
flowers burning like candles in a deathroom.

After the Final Skin Graft

I awakened on my belly—my back, a raw field from nape to heels. Nev
lawn the kids couldn't play on, thickening

Jello which mustn't be moved. Even the sheets kept away,
draped on a wire Quonset, a heat lamp curing me like wheat.

The burn unit was suddenly explicit: doctors I'd thought
were cruel were actually kind. No more scalpels

lurked behind their eyes. And I *saw* the curtains, benign
cascade of secular flowers, the plastic wall, dimpled

like a plucked goose. I would never be whole.

My coal-dead fingertips were wrenched from bone,
my arms marbled like salt meat, but I was no longer stuck

on the churn of my back. The turn from torture was light
particles clearing from mist. I drank cup after cup of Red Rose tea,

lifted to the taste of mountains, bitter flush
of a world I'd reenter like a wind-drift seed.

Learning to Fly

When I am stroked by the dark
hand of melancholy, when I can't move or when I move against

myself, I can say, *Now Dion. Levitate!*
My mother taught me this, my whole body,

flattened into the filth
of the wall-to-wall, the thin wiry whip whipping me. I was amazed

how the sharpness was always sharper than I thought it would be—
sharper than I remembered it. I became devout, felt great sympathy

for the backs of my knees, the insides
of my elbows, the exposed nape. It was a kind of pushing

into visions. I saw myself as tender, pink-skinned baby
rat or new puppy, eyes gluey, crawling blind.

When I was five, my mother pulled down
my soiled panties, rubbed my face in the stool. My disgust

was so much more than I expected
as she slowly and carefully smeared it around my lips, showing me

how living in a human body is creature. Something embedded under
my skin unfolded from my blades, released. I was lifted up.

The day my sister visited the burn ward

was the day the handsome orderlies tubbed me
in the wrong cleanser.
I wanted to feel clean,
but I felt like flames.
She said, *Don't complain,*
you're finally getting attention.

She was right—I craved attention
except when being tubbed
by handsome orderlies, who let me complain
as they dumped in caustic cleanser,
scoured my stubbed tips lost to flames
because I had to be clean.

If I wasn't clean,
if they didn't pay attention,
debride my hips flattened by flames,
if I wasn't tubbed,
puss and fibrin cut with cleanser—
I wouldn't live to complain.

I fever-raved, couldn't stop complaining,
didn't care if I was clean,
disdained the handsome orderlies, their cleanser,
their wire scrubbers, their attention
twice a day, sloughed and tubbed
again and again in flames.

So many ways to flame.
Even freezing wet, hoisted back to air, I'd complain—

my unsheathed flesh, bone-cold above the tub,
before a Percocet, sheets smooth and clean
helped me shift my attention.
But that day, I sizzled from the cleanser.

Dear Sister, on the day you visited—what a terrible cleanser
they cast in the water. Smell of iron, ruby red as flames.
I couldn't give you my attention, just complained,
teeth knocking, eyes back-rolling, after they lifted me clean
from the burning tub.

Nasturtiums

I

Then the ground was lit
by a sprawl of them—
lily pad leaves,
spiced, sticky bloom,
a flame rushing the field.

II

Then at home, a spark
struck me. My robe caught.
The belt was knotted, so I rose
as smoke above the roar.

III

Then the doctors peeled
what skin remained, laid pieces
of my parchment on the plains
of grainy muscle.

(My breasts and back they wrapped
in corpses' skin.)

IV

Months later, I gazed at my face—
bland, glazed with the grace
of morphine—my body,
thin limbed, bent,
fingernails, crumbly as coal.

V

Behind my eyes, still,
the beaded leaves,
veined, shot with light.
Blossoms like bright mouths—
the needle-sweet tongues.

Posies

I was a botched child
in a land where children fell
from the sky like snow, were left
unguarded for wounded lions.

I ran around with a net,
placed butterflies in jars.
Like old parents, they softened and died.

Pinning a thorax in a box
was my payback
for suffering, a way to stay alive.

Oh, childhood is a crown
worn forever—

holding hands with friends, I spun,
screaming songs
with no apparent meaning.

You see, hundreds of years ago,
there was a plague.
Dogs ate the dead out of pits.
Children can't stop singing about it.

3.

The Ranch

Manure slurry, foundered hooves,
saber saws, bandsaws,

pulleys with no purpose
hanging in the sway-backed shed,

mad pony, ready to buck, deep through the heart
with a muscled neck, side-eye pony,

ready to brain me
when he bolts beneath the tulip tree.

Herd goats bell at the riverbank,
pumas haunt the shadows, stashed nutshells

molder in heaps,
smelling of virus and pee.

A mastiff named Tiny waits
in the field, lazy and tripwired for blood.

I can feel how he loves me
like an assassin loves a slow dance.

His devotion shimmers the bees.

I take my faithless body there, enter
with the safety of stars.

This is where a child asks herself:
Why are you sad?

Paris

Because I was smallest in a line of four,
descending in strength and size: Father, Mother, Sister, Me,
because I sat beneath an ironing board reading *The Wizard of Oz*
and held time's center close like holding a dog in a spinning house,
because my mother feared the religious who spoke in tongues,
and I became aware of my tongue,
called envelopes *antelopes* and the twisting whip *angel in the sky*
because, with every beating, I rebirthed into dagger light,
learned to shut the door behind me,
lie on pink concrete with a snake's happiness of warmth,
because there were bobcats and coyotes in the mustard field,
we saw each other and the electric seconds never left me,
because I could startle away from pain with a red tail's cry,
was taught to kill fifty rabbits in a single afternoon,
saw their lungs and kidneys tunneled for air and blood,
because I thought of Paris, the miserable sewers
where children survived,
I felt the hush and flow of organs, the glow
of meat. My crystal bones.

Right & Left

If she lives, she'll lose her left hand and right foot.
                    —The burn surgeon to my mother

You should have seen it—like a panther
dropped from a tree—
fire clenched my back.

You should have seen it—right foot
seared the wall-to-wall—fearless advance
toward the tub to flood the flame.

Then my left hand took control
flung the robe—
like a sensei flings a burning ball of Chi.

Right foot blood-stepped to the phone.
Left hand dialed—
skin like peels of cooked potato,
lifted from its starch.

If she lives. If she lives.
They meant I'd die. Or gain a terrible symmetry—
Stump-club, right. Twist-stub, left.

But I kept my hand and foot—
fingers blunted, webs across the left-hand palm,
right sole neatly meshed and mended.

Artists, soldiers, dancers, angels—
quick without thought,
the body wields its helpers.

Right step, right, winch the devil off the back.
Left hand, left, throw him away—

Blessing the Burn

So when I stood in flame
I centered in its eye
and when my skin
and then my muscle
phased to air I felt
the commandments of organ and bone
and when the ambulance rolled in I saw
its jumbled white suns trading places
its whine pressing the sky
too late too late
then I saw an old friend drove it
he whispered my name like a saint's
Oh in that moment I knew
the world saw me
then the long-slow began
a grume a rindless mass
but finally from my feet
where she'd worked for eternity
to thread a needle
where my skin was whole
a woman stood she was the first
to hunt a speckless vein
Oh she mired me
in the surge of a blue world
its counter currents its careless need
Oh I'd burned I'd burned
hair to heels
but my face
was the unseared seed
of my next life
and my breasts were barely tinged
just sparks around my nipples
like stars

Darkness

Which contains me, which is multitude,
unwrapped gift of space, No
I won't take for an answer,

horse that trots toward me, halter I carry,
my business, my burn on a bent spoon,
my thirst, my well water

that hides itself,
from the fixed and burning stars,
dark sister born with me,

who cannot love me,
but is still sister,
mask and ax, sparrow whistle

of an executioner as he walks to work,
fashionable, familiar, hated—it takes my friends,
thrums my loneliness, fret-lines my face.

Big bang, black hole, in the beginning there was,
first atom of shared loss,
mother of language, mother of song.

Darkness, my mother, pushing me
to the crying light.

Burned Body Contemplates the Bottom Sheets

Not razors, exactly, more like
powdered glass, gunpowder,
asbestos maybe, super glue,
so when I moved, it wrenched
the dendrites of my skin.
I had no skin. I'm sorry.
I had no skin.
What I really mean is
the sheets were slim silver
whips, as slim and silver
as millions of threads, stitching
their silver through
what shouldn't be seen.
The undergarments of flesh
should be secret.
The body is a fruit
that should never be peeled,
never eaten by air,
never touched behind
the thin curtain of its cover.
The sheets were touch.
Not touch. There was no
touch. There was a diamond-
bright rake and flay
I sank from, into the dark-
red halls and caverns
of my guts, to the proper hush
and flow machine
of a living girl.
Breath. Nephron flow

of urine. Pancreas
ooze of insulin. The *wish
wish wish* of the heart
crying itself out
to the sheet,
the sheet holding me.

Station

Sometimes, I wake to the call
of a train, though I know
there is no train.

I think I'm in my old bed,
my childhood house—
house filled with absence,

like a friend drove off a cliff,
or the neighbor shot the horse.
The shock of loss, everyday

in that house, with its stink
of sour milk, grit in the rugs,
fleas, swollen dogs, the bay-window light

falling on an empty chair—
perfect ranch house, blown apart
by bad renovation and neglect.

Now, the rooms are empty
of wailing or song. My old room
is stuffed with a staircase,

my sister's, impossible to enter
through its stuck sliding door.
Our mother lives alone there,

one mother in twenty rooms,
sleeping open-mouthed,
tipped in a La-Z-Boy.

And although I can't love her
for making me crawl
through gauntlets of whips and slaps,

to emerge, each time
like a wet purple infant—
I feel her there, by herself,

in her strange dream of mastiffs
following her through endless rooms,
and I'm the lonely one,

listening to the ghost whistle
of a train leaving
for somewhere else.

This morning, a coyote

paced across our path, laughing at us,
light as a ghost, pink tongue resting
on his teeth. My terrier lost her mind—
chased him to the rocky bottomlands.

I couldn't follow. Could only
hear her scream, buzzards tilting above me.

I covered my ears with my palms,
turned away, ran home.
An hour later, she returned,
limping, covered in punctures.

Isn't the well-worn trail enough?
It loops around the meadow—prick of birdsong,
oaks dripping like metronomes, ancient pines
swimming in mist. I look back at my house,
and its red paint seems joyous.

Am I happy? I gave up predators long ago.
Although one left a tooth in the tender
skin of my neck. Oh, stupid dog, I'll never
blame you, always seeking distractions
in the fabulous stink of pheromones.

Will I meet him again
in a brick-walled espresso house?
An Al-Anon meeting?
Smoking under a gargoyle
outside a wax museum?

I want more of his presents—
envelopes made of ten-dollar bills,
thumb-sized books of mystic poetry,
a sketch of a Möbius strip,
twisted for infinity.

But he escapes. Down the slot canyon.
Stay, Dion. Don't follow.

Pickerel

It seemed I was only told
to favor action verbs
over states of being,
to pump gas and stay out
of the cheap part of town.
There was lots of talk
of how men preferred
debutante smiles, eye gazing,
crossed thighs, voices
like vespers, an absence
of blurted opinions,
high rope strung
between demur and desirable.
How much can a girl bear?
Being loved was an impossible
equation. Even if by a small percentage,
wrong was always wrong—
always five kinds of trouble,
chasing chickens, thinking
I belonged in a red cape,
singing the wrong song
about Casey Jones
and a whorehouse door.
No one told me, I just knew—
adore the pickerel!
Freshets rushing past.
Psalms. The quiet
of my grandfather's hands
as he peeled potatoes
with his folding knife.
I was taken
by a flare of leaves,
a drunken buddha,
whispering *Be, Be, Be.*

Born a Girl

In me lives a mustached man.
He's always the boss,
always swaggers the playground.
In me lives a little man who loves
big men and mean dogs.
I can't help it. I was witness
to a father's hunger. . . sky-wild
for my mother, his fingers rubied for her.
She hanged him like a horse thief,
clipped the foaming stud
he stole for her, made him cry
in a darkened garage.
I wasn't what he wanted...
manchild who'd ride with him,
enter his swinging doors like a god,
pack a mean left hook
back to back in a parking lot.
O little father in lift shoes,
even on your deathbed,
you griped about my sex.
Old man, I admit it, I like you
starting fights and duking it out,
still alive inside me.

After survival, the weight of air

is what awakens you to dazzlement,
the way a monster awakens, caught
in the neck snare of hunger.

Is what a spiderling drifts in, lost—
after it lifts from its birth home—
carried on silk through everything breathed.

Is five million billion tons of sky—
troposphere, holding stratosphere,
holding spheres above it. Wonder

of thunderheads as they cruise through it,
loosen their dense bodies,
unbind their burden of hail.

Most times, you don't notice
the fifteen pounds of pressure
holding your new-skinned need

with the ease of light on a peach's cheek,
ease of lung-bellow and pull, quiet
wind through nostril-hollow

and down the muscle of throat. It is
what enters, what you choose
to quiet or quicken

to the nervous flutter of bird.
Sometimes, you forget you're breathing.
Yet, soft, you breathe. Sometimes

you forget you are touched.
Yet you are touched.

Faith

The final verse is always the trees.
—Joy Harjo

My belief in god was improvised
from the song of a thousand birds
clustered in a jack pine at sunset,
the limbs stark against scarlet streaks
opening like veins in the sky.

In silence, trees
count years looping within
their persistent bodies—
parched or swollen lineations,
ancient scripture of shadow,
drought and fire, plagues of sawflies.

This field circled by oaks
is burdened with spirits. People
walk barefoot over acorns,
reach into barbed brambles,
press their cheeks to bark,
exhale history into fog.

The year my twins were born,
I planted two maples here,
their height and girth, another way
to catch time in flesh and sapwood.

Minor gods of wind and light
tangle in their branches. Leaves
capture dew and drip—
a loud clock keeping me awake,
wondering what will outlive me.

4.

Wolf Moon

10 January 2020

Night when wolves howl in the chill,
in the maddening jade-white light,
night when the moon swims above the hill,
its face streaked by stark trees.

For millennia, we've heard them ravening
outside our villages, our flesh aching
with their lament, their hunger, the warmth
they find inside the tender throat of prey.

Whimpers, wine blood, swollen
shadow, night sharpened, hearts taken
beneath the cold love of moon—
Do we sense the sadness

of the apex predator? Oh, I think any animal
who mates for life knows loneliness.

Hidden

From the baselines in Big Sister's
bedroom, from the longhairs
necking with her
in the backseat of the Lincoln
or stuck together
like dolphins in the deep end,
I knew something of sex,
but I suffered
a nervy pulse I couldn't decipher.
Wires crossed and fizzed.
Their crux flickered
a teensy bulb, center front
of my hairless cleft—
crowning bitty head
in a wimply fold,
tight whorl that needed
soothing, clenchy itch
that pressed me to straddle
the edge of my third-grade chair,
glide side to side on a hidden pin.
When Mummy saw me press
my fingers to my need, her lip curled
with what looked like desire.
She pronounced me *Soiled. Dirty.*
Still, as I sipped my tea
in bone china with bloody roses,
as I looked at the naked
ceiling pulse, I pushed
my center fire, poked and poked
to keep it quiet.
When I lay down, it grew louder.

Some Guy

I'd agreed to this coupling
in his closet-sized room—
because he was named Guy, and I liked
the idea of that: *My first guy*
was named Guy, I would say,
like a child's excuse
for breaking something.
He was my next-door neighbor
at Pleasure Point. Surfing
had shaped his trapezius
like flesh wings. This also stirred me.
I think I thought men closed
the wounds in a woman's body,
but when it happened, I felt the ache
of seeing the moon up close
through a telescope,
knowing I'd never touch it.
My mind wandered as he
drilled and pumped.
I thought of irrigation pipes
I'd jammed together on the ranch,
then pulled apart with a twist
to move to a different field.
The next day, he saw me
in my yard lifting a trellis.
I knew—it was almost telepathic—
if I raised my arms, he'd be cruel.
Your armpits are too wide,
he said and walked away.
I felt like a vase in the home
of a hoarder when I needed
to be prized on a mantle.
Proud of itself. Picked up and polished.
If I couldn't be that, I wanted to shatter.

Wolf

I'm trying to forget a man
I don't want to forget.
He could harp the strings of my body
with his spacetime eyes.

You could be a dancer, he said, and I danced.
You could be a sparrow, he said, and I sang.

Now, I see the curve of his back,
the half moons of his fingernails
in river rocks and languishing clouds.
Even my clothes, pulled from a lonely closet,
ask his permission.

I think I was pretty once,
but there was something tragic about me.
I had that pale kind of skin, wan,
as if most of me were mist.

And that man I want to forget—
I think my deer eyes stirred him.
I think they made him want to open
his wounds like a trap door.

I have loved him ever since.
That's what happens sometimes—
you meet a stranger, hand him
a basket of mint and clean fruit.

You're taken, warm inside him,
then ripped out.

North

I can't recline the driver's seat,
so I sit straight-backed
like a guru,

crack a window,
the air fresh
as a silver needle.

I pass the bald head
of Shasta, that dormant god,
pass the rust-colored pines
eaten by fire.

Back home, my mother's
asleep, the space heater ticking
at her feet.

She's ninety-five and cold.
From feeling no love,
the doctor says,

and I wonder if he means she
feels no love for anyone, or
she feels no love from me

because I don't love her,
despite the years
of meals and clean socks,
free education and down payments.

Now I hear the poets tell me I must
bear witness
to the smell and sound

of her big-boned hands
as she erased me.

But I'd rather go north,
say amen to my lack
of gratitude,
sing hallelujah to this great
emptiness

as I move closer and closer
to the coldest place on Earth.

Peacock

All Leif's punk friends hated me
with my mullet and sellout job,
no skin-tight glamor, no heroin pallor.
I followed his band around Seattle
like an orphan follows a stand-in dad,
prayed a wave of energy might
pass through him, a God particle
oscillate his bones enough to feel me.

But then, Oh victory! He took a walk with me—
the night, full of wind, a storm
lifting water from Lake Washington
like it might become sky and drown us.

He wrapped me in his arms,
said I was his girlfriend,
drove me home on his motorcycle.
To his bed! Then fell asleep
without touching me.
And so it went for many years.

There's more to the story,
but I like best how much I craved him,
second best, how much I hated him
when he took a second woman.
I like to savor my fevered jealousy
when he stole my peacock feathers,
gifted them to her like a bouquet,
how he let me smell her perfume
on his sweater, watched me
scream my dirtiest epithets
as he fingered his guitar.

It was forty years ago, my anger tore
like a fire break against a greater flame.
I like to think I'll never
burn like that again. But I could.

It's never too late to believe
a beautiful story, start a war
to keep it true.

Mariana

Why do I drift on memories?
Conjure what I lost, repeat
the loss again and again?

Is it because of a happiness
that rises in me like heat
or fog touched by sun?

It weakens me, invades my skin—
the hope I can hold on
to anything, even my bones.

I heard there was a time when
poets returned to marble tombs
with shovels and axes

to exhume their beloveds—
Emerson's young bride, two years gone,
held again in his arms.

How many times have I returned
to a mother who savaged me?
Searched for her again and again

in the bodies of men—their eyes,
burnished like hers as she beat me—
blood prick of a needle, then bliss

as I recut memory's diamond.

Have you heard of light organs
in creatures who live at such depth,
sunlight refuses to enter?

Luminous glands embed in their skin.
Only in the sea, only in silent
darkness, the sting of salt.

Seattle Freeze 1978

I walked The Ave with it tucked in my raincoat—
the paperback Yeats

bought at a second-hand bookstore on NE 42nd
with an occult name like The Alchemist

or Dark Magician, carried it
like a stone tablet, back to my tribe

of one, studied it
in the smoke-filled coffee shop,

full of young men moving chess pieces
in the precise way of surgeons, intent

over someone else's heart.

I sat in a pew that faced a wall
inscribed with lovers' names

and anarchy signs, at my feet
blue-bottle flies face-up

like chips of bornite crystal.

The barista was a beautiful,
unhappy woman. Everyone was in thrall

of her long black hair and sullen eyes.
One man with skin masses on his nose

like the Ghirlandaio
handed her fancy-cut paper snowflakes.

After he left, she placed them on saucers
under grandes, which I drank one after the other,

Styx-dark, bitter and burning, fraying
my nervous system and making me needy.

I wanted to meet someone
who liked my legs and listened to me.

Instead, I went to dinner alone
in one of those '70s diners

with tahini dressing and grainy rolls,
the radiant pregnant waitresses carrying beans and soup

like doulas attending my sorrow.

Seattle seemed full of Nordic stock,
more robust than I and saner:

I was California bred, stupid as an umbrella.

How strange it all seems now: those heavy days,
store windows piled high with antiques no one bought,

the shopkeepers who let me have what I wanted
for nothing. They must have been lonely,

or maybe they loved the blueish, sun-starved
skin beneath my eyes.

At night, I feared my attic room:
books stacked in corners,

brown pennies in jars, my clothes—too many
for the closet,

just warm-weather cottons,
and the whole world, silent and cold.

In Bellingham

I lived in a shanty on a ridge, one window
        facing the Salish Sea, the other,
a stand of cedars, their scaly leaves,
        a ceaseless ticking on my roof.
I'd charmed a man to let me live there.
        He fished in Alaska, June
to September, placed the keys in my hand
        like a velvet bag of diamonds.
He was in love with me, but I didn't want him.
        He hustled mushrooms, hung drywall,
never learned to read or write,
        but could fix anything,
stooped over the motor of his Model A,
        his bare back, muscled and pelted,
fingers light on the implements,
        as he murmured, *Rich to the right. Lean to the left.*
At the time, I was in love with a Seattle man
        who designed high-rise towers made of glass.
I'd moved north to escape the sight of him
        with his red-haired girlfriend,
her sun-flecked skin and slender arms.
        Nights, I'd hike home slow up Sehome hill,
my body hot inside the steamy wool,
        the double-coated nylon of my coat.
When I got home, the cabin was cold,
        quiet. I'd bank the fire, fall asleep
thinking about those two men—
        one who dropped me off for good
on a dark street. The other, wordless,
        his eyes stitched with light.

Defects

My daughter visits a shrink, who argues with her
about my ex-boyfriend—whether he was a *blot*
or a *stain* on my children's life.

My daughter says *blot*. The shrink says *stain*.
I feel sorry for this bollixed professional.
What can he say about my heat

for a man whose fists flexed like my father's?
Who saw my children as rivals,
left lip-smears of toothpaste
caked on their Barney towels.

I give the shrink the benefit. Say, *Yeah, stain* because
some memories never wash out. They travel
through generations like sickle-cell, hemophilia,
blood-blemish, stigmata.

It's enough to make me believe
the Christians—sin's an apple, and no spitting out.

No wonder the millennia of pilgrims
walking on their knees, tendering lilies
to a motherly statue, no wonder
the black-robed crones troubling rosaries.

But, I'm no Christian, I know there's no
absolution for letting a man live with us
like a squatter, a man who
crumped my ass while I cooked
his charred steaks, who stockpiled guns
like he wanted to shoot up a church.

My daughter looked it up—*blot*
is the same as *stain*, she tells me calmly.
She knows exactly what I did.

Expulsion

I have a cashmere poncho and a beautiful son,
a husband who watches my shadow
as we walk, sees a nimbus
crowning my head.

My daughter is a bird. She hoots
night into my ear.

I've been carried over and over
to the creek like meat to be cleaned
before eating,
been in double jeopardy,
sinned the same way more than twice   ,
been exonerated due to luck and money.

Let me put it this way: I was deviled
by my childhood. My sister would beg
to beat me. I was an animal
my mother ate to fortify her blood.

So I mistook the punctures in my throat
the sudden energy of lovers
when they walked out
as a kind of marriage. I felt bedecked in white
the very center of attention

until the pump and surge of blood
flooded my lace.

How did I change? Not choice—
more like lightning taken by a tree.

I neglected the itch to bolt
when I wasn't the feast,
stopped believing Paradise is a place
I used to live.

Pussy Neck Ode

Vagina neck. Twat gullet.
Neck with brain wrinkles
that yank me from hallucinations
of my unsagged past.
Pussy neck, you reveal
what was hidden—
secret winkle, tide-flower, fuzz-dimple
I learned to love, pet
I forget to look at for years,
Jello-junk I still squeeze
before I fall asleep.
How did you travel up my country,
land at my neck
complicate the frontier between
chin and throat? Oh, folly—
thinking my parts
are singular. That my baby hatch,
my eentsy twig of split second
joy, my pee whistle
are different from
any other piece of me.
I should have known—
the puss is not strange.
Not unique. She knew
the sister snatch—
the similar mouth, ruby-
split with lips and spit,
the other tunnels—
one so close—
of sleek and diverse

pleasure, all leading
to the deep of me.
Pussy neck, you puckered,
just at the moment
when the spiced bloodlet,
the moon-timed harvest,
the leak-out from the empty
sac finally ceased, when age-
heat flushed me. Oh, pussy neck,
flower below my face, last blossom
of the drooped vine. Trail
of the body's falling star.

Mid Century

Then a boy kissed me.

I loved how he'd leap a fence, disappear,
then drop from a tree with stolen art.

Blues LPs I'd never heard of—

Percy Mayfield, Johnny Otis,
a sound that proved suffering

stayed after suffering ended.

I loved the theft—coffee table books, soapstone statu-
ettes,
small flutes of whittled wood.

I loved the way he wouldn't change,

and the way I did
because of what he gave me.

Yes, I loved his skin

when it vanished into greenery,
returned with the smell

of acacia and salt.
I loved how he trembled

like a small box of music.
Open your hand, he'd say. *I have a gift.*

Springtime: The Dog Jumps on the Bed and Bites You as We Fuck, and I Feel Young Again

Sometimes, I prayed: *Jesus,*
Let me sin again. I couldn't help it.
Look at the iconography of my tribe—
long-hairs nailed up like rock stars;
saints, starving like haute models, half naked,
full of arrows; the royal-blue beauty
of the crying Mother, her arms crossed
over a bleeding heart, like the single mom

I once was, bored of my kids, tired
of staring at the slide, waiting
for an accident. An eye watched me all day
as I bathed the filthy,
added cheese to dimpled wafers.
Night bulged, darker than water.

But today, the house is quiet, just you
and the meddlesome dog, whining
like an archangel. Kick her off,
lock her out. She can pester the door.
Babe, let's start over. I'll pull you in—
my old body, dry as a copperhead.

Let's fight with pitted eyes and razor spurs,
then sleep into each other,
until we're grafted apple trees—
the softness of our petals
becoming wind.

Geese

I do my best, genuflect
  at the stations of the cross:
    refuse the Florida grapefruit
after a dose of statins.

I apply myself: say no thanks
  to the hot toddy,
    the divorce lawyer,
the partisan argument.

I sit cross-legged at the feet of tea gurus,
  pour Gung Fu Pu-erh,
    enter the sunlight
stored in liquid amber.

I watch birds, their love affairs,
  the grackle in my maple
    swelling his feathers
at an indifferent mate.

I do these things & they sustain
the dark bones that carry me

because all beings cling
  to instinct and habit—
    church bells, morning coffee,
the urn of incense

because if I perform each of these
  small sacraments, I won't lift
    into the light of spring,
turn my body into a small arrow of flight,

too high to see.
      I won't become an unraveling skein
            pointed north.
The glittering wings:

are they glass? Or has the sun
            turned them to diamonds?

Accidental Fuck

Zipless. Uncontrollable.
Then you wake
from some sweaty, unconscionable—
yet somewhat enjoyable—
night-time rollick.

You pull into the curve
of your husband's body, unroused
by your churning, your calling out,
your nighttime prowling
in the flop houses and titty dives
of your subconscious,

where you do it with your bland colleagues
who wear button-up shirts
lined like graph paper,
with your silly-putty students,
your red-hot riding teacher,
with his big hands,
padded and seamed like a baseball glove,
or that one time with your
transgender cousin.

All their dicks, so enormous,
you can't refrain from gripping them,
their girth like the flesh handle
of a hammer you keep pounding
on the cruel nail of your need.

And the astonishment every time
at the sight of it swelling,
its measured intensity

like something born in time lapse,
the goat-like tumescence,
friendly, yet so clearly impersonal.

Maybe you just like how it feels—
after you've been taken
by the vortex forbidden —
to wake up, beached
on the warm sands of relief,
on the Ithaca of commitment,
your husband's snores
gusting through your hair
like an offshore wind.

How to Dress Wounds

Insist on entering cathedrals,
the window colors
sliding through flesh. Feel them,
clockless, the centuries
laboring toward god filling you
like breath. Remember:
what happens,
happens slowly. Listen
to something small as a butterfly
shivering the back of your skull.

Look at your unmanageable body
as the plant sees the sun, complete
devotion. Day after day, drag yourself
to the same altar, drink and eat
as best you can. Forgive

the imperfections on the skin of fruits,
the unblessed meat. Awaken
to light moving through curtains.

Sleep the way horses canter
through dark trees, riderless

until they forget they're horses.

Dear Tongue,

I like the way you tender the inner flesh of cheek,
bend to touch your hinge in the red-flesh crevice of your cave.
I love the way you play with folds along the inner base of gum,
pester and pester the zippery edge of a chipped tooth.
Oh, you want so much! You want to repent, but first transgress,
to scrape sweet apple, lick the way a candle licks.
Oh, worship tongue, whet-stone tongue, tongue that loves
the sweat off a hip bone, god tongue who speaks in tongues,
I like it when you roll your rhymes and tap my palate. Whistle tongue,
song tongue, umbrage tongue, you've led me down some catnip alleys,
probed some chancy ears. But now, don't you think it right
to lick the midnight caruncle of desire? Dear slab of pink
who screamed my first hello, you will whisper my last goodbye.
My last *Please, please, scratch between my shoulder blades.*

Hunger Moon

February 9, 2020

watches us fast while the world freezes,
while game is thin, and there's nothing

to eat in the lingering winter
but a fatless rabbit and a dirty root.

Storm Moon, Snow Moon we say—
but this year, sun for weeks. Dry wind

downs a power line, sets a pine ablaze,
no rain, no cloak of morning frost,

no meadow grass bent beneath a crystal sheet.
But isn't this a hunger? A longing for winter

so deep, my bones feel like dust, my gut
hollow, waiting for the rhythm of rainfall

swept from the windshield as I drive downtown
to buy Picuda oil, shade coffee, Chilean grapes.

Hunger Moon, I want it all—the tap on the flue,
the wood stove fueled by a wet-fallen oak,

the thrill moment of takeoff,
droplets on my window pushed back by a great force.

Even in summer, when the garden's a reckless mess
of cress and fat-bottom squash—

Hunger Moon, you follow me.

Acknowledgments

American Journal of Poetry: "Born a Girl," "Learning to Fly"

Anti-Heroin Chic: "Presidential Campaign 2020"

B O D Y: "Pussy Neck Ode"

Book of Matches: "Paris," "Sheep Shear," "I Wanted Boys"

Catamaran Literary Quarterly: "Peacock"

Chautauqua: "Hunger Moon"

Cave Wall: "Blessing the Burn," "Seattle Freeze 1979"

Chiron: "Wolf Moon"

Cincinnati Review: "Posies"

Gingerbread: "Wolf"

Massachusetts Review: "Helpless"

Missouri Review: "The Ranch"

Nailed: "Closet," "Roots," "This Morning a Coyote"

Narrative: "After Survival, the Weight of Air," "After the Final Skin Graft," "Big Sister," "Burned Body Contemplates the Bottom Sheet," "Fallen," "Time in the Burn Ward"

MacQueens Quinterly: "In Bellingham," "Red Truck"

Poets Reading the News: "There was smoke in the sunrise"

Porter Gulch Review: "Faith," "How to Dress Wounds"

Quiddity: "Eyes Round Sockets With No Light"

RHINO: "Mid Century"

Rogue Agent: "What It Took"

Salamander: "Plenty"

Salt: "Pickerel"

San Pedro River Review: "North"

Sequestrum: "World Books"

Slipstream: "Small Murders"

South Florida Poetry Journal: "Station"

SWWIM: "Hidden," "Nasturtiums"

Trampoline: "Darkness," "Geese,"

What Rough Beast (Indolent Books): "Accidental Fuck," "Big Fish Eat Little Fish," "Mariana," "Okanogan 1980," "Springtime: The Dog Jumps on the Bed and Bites You As We Fuck, and I Feel Young Again"

Valparaiso Poetry Review: "The man who bathed me in the burn ward"

"Expulsion" was reprinted in the *Marin Center Anthology*.

"Some Guy" was reprinted in the anthology *Sh!t Men Say to Me*.

"After Survival, the Weight of Air," "After the Final Skin Graft," "Big Sister," "Burned Body Contemplates the Bottom Sheet," "Time in the Burn Ward" were republished in *Spoonie*.

"After Survival, the Weight of Air," "After the Final Skin Graft," "Big Sister," "Burned Body Contemplates the Bottom Sheet," "Time in the Burn Ward" were finalists in the Narrative Poetry Prize.

"After the Final Skin Graft," won an Honorable Mention in the Winning Writers Margaret Reid Poetry Prize for Traditional Verse

---

Thank you to the following people who supported me during the creation of *Sadness of the Apex Predator*.

Michael, my husband, often my first reader, and if the poem is bad enough, my only reader. He deserves the biggest thanks of all.

For his close reading of the manuscript and consideration of each poem, Kwame Dawes.

Ellen Bass, although she was not the first to tell me I could be a writer, she was the first I believed. Ellen is very convincing!

To my California writing buddies, JoAnn Birch, Kim Schliebauer, Julie Murphy, Julia Chiapella, Erin Redfern, Julia Levine, and Francesca Bell, and to my Bellingham Village Books writing workshop, specifically Joy Wright and Bob Lazlow for keeping the group alive. A special shoutout goes to John Green for welcoming me.

Fanaz Fatemi, Julie Murphy, Julia Chiapella, Roxi Power, and Geneffa Jahan of The Hive, thank you for your dedication. Sometimes, I can't believe what five womyn can accomplish!

To the many poets I have interviewed on *The Hive Poetry Collective Podcast*: these conversations have been invaluable to my growth.

For Rooja Mohassessy, Erin Belieu, Denise Duhamel, and Jessica Cuello, a special thank you for excellent conversation and thoughtful blurbs.

For sharing the Mystery, I thank my students.

To Catherine Segurson and the Catamaran Literary Reader, for bringing me into the fold.

Sincere appreciation to the folks at Cornerstone Press who made this book possible: Dr. Ross Tangedal, Ellie Atkinson, Chloe Cieszynski, Sophie McPherson, Natalie Reiter, and Ava Willett.

And then there's Danusha Laméris and Vinty Barsodi, what can I say? They make me feel like a crazy kid, and what could be better than that?

And always, to the Muse, which is life itself.

DION O'REILLY is the author of *Ghost Dogs* (2020). Her poems and essays have appeared in *Rattle, The Sun, American Journal of Poetry, Cincinnati Review, Narrative, The New Ohio Review, The Massachusetts Review*, and *New Letters*. She splits her time between a ranch in California's Santa Cruz Mountains and her residence in Bellingham, Washington.